The cause.

THE (ALMOST) COMPLEAT ANGLER

OR PROOF THAT THERE IS MORE TO FISHING THAN JUST CATCHING FISH

TIMOTHY BENN

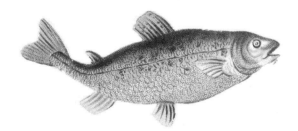

LONDON
VICTOR GOLLANCZ LTD
1985

First published in Great Britain 1985
by Victor Gollancz Ltd,
14 Henrietta Street, London WC2E 8QJ

Text and arrangement
© Timothy Benn 1985

Designed by Jonathan Newdick

Typeset in England by Dorchester Typesetting Group Ltd.
Printed in Italy by Arnoldo Mondadori Editore

British Library Cataloguing in Publication Data

Benn, Timothy
    The (almost) compleat angler.
    1. Fishing—History—Pictorial works
    I. Title
    799.1'2   SH421

    ISBN 0-575-03713-X

ACKNOWLEDGEMENTS

The majority of material appearing in this book is reproduced from items in the author's own collection. Every effort has been made to trace holders' copyrights and to give due acknowledgement. The diversity of material included in the book however is such that there may be omissions, for which the author craves indulgence.

The author and publisher would like to thank the following people for giving permission to include illustrations which are their copyright:

The Master and Fellows of Brasenose College, Oxford for the portrait of Dr Alex Nowel; the President of the Flyfishers' Club, London for the Club's library bookplate and material from its *Journal*; the trustees of the estate of the late C. F. Tunnicliffe for illustrations from *Going Fishing*; the proprietors of *Punch* for cartoons from that illustrious magazine; David and Charles Ltd for material from Gamages' 1906 catalogue; Dover Publishing Inc, New York for Bewick illustrations; The House of Hardy for material from its catalogues; Webb and Bower Ltd for illustrations by the Rev. W. Houghton; the proprietors of the *Illustrated London News* for Spy cartoons; the executors of the estate of the late Agnes Miller Parker for engravings from *Down the River*; Raphael Tuck for early 20th century postcards and scraps. Blackie and Son Ltd for the illustration by Frank Adams.

Practical help has been provided in many other ways and I am especially grateful to John Simpson who read, and copiously corrected, my first typescript and to Christine Terry who typed it. My thanks are due also to David Beazley for providing important material; to the Clarke-Hall Bookshop, London, from whom I have acquired much angling ephemera over the years; and to Jonathan Newdick for his patience and skill in designing the book. I also acknowledge permission to use material from Mr Gamage's Great Toy Bazaar 1902-1906 published by Denys Ingram Ltd. The illustrations from *The Tale of Mr Jeremy Fisher* which appear on page 12 are reprinted by permission of the publishers.

CONTENTS

Two boys fishing. A charming hand-coloured print. The initials in the bottom right hand corner indicate that the artist was probably George Morland (1763–1804).

INTRODUCTION

'I. Thes. 4.II Study to be quiet.' Thus Izaak Walton concluded in the last paragraph of the second, much enlarged edition of *The Compleat Angler*, published in 1655. When that masterly work was written remains a matter of conjecture, but the first edition was published in 1653. Other editions followed in quick succession, most notably the fifth, which contained Charles Cotton's contribution. This has since become the most reprinted book in the English language after the Bible. What joy and delight it has brought to generations of anglers as a result.

But then angling is not just a pastime or pursuit; it is an obsession bordering on fanaticism. Indeed your true angler can only be described as an addict.

It is not surprising therefore, that angling, of which Izaak Walton is regarded as the 'father', has become the world's largest participant sport. Over the years its adherents have been numbered not just in hundreds of thousands, but in millions. Nor should it be surprising that amongst so many folk, so much ingenuity and craftsmanship should have been shown. This has applied as equally to the impedimenta of angling as to the tactics and techniques of fishing itself. Around angling a sizeable industry has been sustained over the years to meet the angler's needs for tackle and equipment. Additionally print, in every conceivable form, has been produced with angling as its theme.

It is some of these strands which this book is intended to chart, not in any definitive sense, but simply to highlight pictorially both the diversity and the skills which have been brought to bear on angling over the centuries and to show how angling has been reflected in literature, art and humour. Because so much contemporary material exists, a somewhat arbitrary cut-off point of about 1950 has been taken in selecting material for inclusion.

All of which goes to show that angling is not simply the contemplative man's recreation, beloved of old Izaak Walton, but that, as the motto of The Flyfishers' Club of London bears witness, *Piscator non solum piscatur*, or roughly translated 'There is more to fishing than just catching fish'.

Go softly by that river-side, or when you would depart,
You'll find it's ever winding tied and knotted round your heart.

Rudyard Kipling
The Prairie

THE ORIGINS OF ANGLING

Whether angling is a sport or a pastime is open to endless debate. In any event, its origins lie deep in antiquity. William Radcliffe, the great angling historian, recorded in the second revised edition of *Fishing from the Earliest Times* (1926) that the first definitive mention of angling is to be found in the tombs of the ancient Egyptians around 2000BC and ascribes to them the first use of the fishing rod. According to Radcliffe, the Assyrians (perhaps better known by schoolboys everywhere for coming down like wolves on the fold) were keen anglers. Many angling scenes were found depicted on the walls of Pompeii and the works of the classic Greek poets contain many references to fishing. Indeed the oldest book on the subject is probably the *Halieutica* of Oppian, the Greek poet.

The first printed book to appear in England on sport was *The Book of Hawking, Hunting and Blasing of Arms* which was published in 1486. Ten years later a second edition was printed, with an additional section specifically devoted to fishing, entitled *The Treatyse of Fysshynge wyth an Angle*. This was produced by Wynkyn Worde, Caxton's successor as publisher and printer at 'the reed pale' in the Almonry of Westminster Abbey.

So much is fact. Beyond that controversy has reigned for many years. Both books were traditionally ascribed to Dame Juliana Berners though scholarship has now determined that no such person existed. Further, both works were often collectively described as *The Boke of St Albans*, though scholars have latterly proved that no connection with that town exists either!

LEFT
A float fisherman as depicted in 1496 in *The Treatyse of Fysshynge wyth an Angle*.

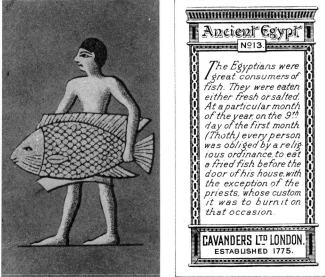

Ancient Egypt No. 13.

The Egyptians were great consumers of fish. They were eaten either fresh or salted. At a particular month of the year, on the 9th day of the first month (Thoth) every person was obliged by a religious ordinance, to eat a fried fish before the door of his house, with the exception of the priests, whose custom it was to burn it on that occasion.

CAVANDERS LTD LONDON.
ESTABLISHED 1775.

Portrait of Dr Alexander Nowel hung in the Hall of Brasenose
College, Oxford.

Dr Nowel was briefly principal of Brasenose College, Oxford, in
1595. His portrait (RIGHT) hangs to this day in the College hall. The
remarkably fine fishing hooks in the picture apparently signify that
Dr Nowel was not only a keen angler but regarded himself as a
'fisher of men'. The invention of bottled beer has been ascribed to
Dr Nowel who was fond of taking a bottle of ale on fishing
expeditions and noticed that it went fizzy after prolonged
immersion in cold water.

BELOW

One print from a collection titled 'Severall Wayes of Hunting,
Hawking and Fishing according to the English Manner invented by
Francis Barlow, etched by W. Hollar' engraved title, and 12 plates,
'And are to be sould by John Overton at the White Horse without
Newgate. London, 1671.'

LEFT

A cigarette card issued by Cavanders Ltd. of London illustrating life
in Ancient Egypt.

THE YOUNG ANGLER

A stick, a piece of string, a bobbin, a bent pin, plus a jam jar secured round the neck with string is how early angling has invariably been portrayed over the centuries. The catch too is predictable – a Minnow (or Penk to old Izaak Walton), a stickleback or Miller's thumb.

And still the fair conceit I'd hold
That fishermen never grow old,
That with the daffodil's gold,
That, with the cowslip's plenty,
And with the loud and building rooks
The man of rods and lines and hooks
Is always one-and-twenty.

Patrick R. Chalmers

'A Wily Angler Watching his Red Float'. From an oil painting by J. C. Hook RA (1819-1907).

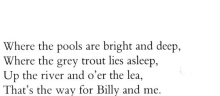

BELOW
'Angling, Old Age, and Youth'. From a charming lithograph in colour by I. Giles after a painting by James Inskipp (1790-1868).

RIGHT
'The Contemplative Boy's Recreation', an engraving by Robert Pollard (1755-1838).

Where the pools are bright and deep,
Where the grey trout lies asleep,
Up the river and o'er the lea,
That's the way for Billy and me.

Why the boys should drive away
Little sweet maidens from their play,
Or love to banter and fight so well,
That's the thing I never could tell.

But this I know, I love to play
Through the meadow, among the hay,
Up the water and o'er the lea,
That's the way for Billy and me.

James Hogg (1772-1835)

THE YOUNG ANGLER

Nothing in children's literature could arouse the budding angler's enthusiasm more strongly than *The Tale of Mr Jeremy Fisher*, written by Beatrix Potter and first published in 1906. The tale brilliantly captures all the themes of angling. The cold of the water's edge, impending boredom, the surge of anticipation at the bite, the extremes of excitement during the ensuing battle with an unseen 'monster' and the very mixed emotions at its loss – only to be instantly superceded (shades of the latter day *Jaws*) by the terror of the hunter himself becoming the hunted. But all's well that ends well with the consolation of a comforting dinner, old friends and the inevitable retelling of the days' events.

It is not recorded whether Beatrix Potter was herself an angler but the *Tale* is told with the precision of someone totally familiar with all the passions of the true fisher – as indeed she should have been, having frequently accompanied her father on angling holidays at Dunkeld on the River Tay.

In later life Beatrix Potter accompanied her husband on fishing trips on a tarn above Near Sawrey in Cumberland, to which she moved from London seven years after writing *The Tale of Mr Jeremy Fisher*. The punt used on these trips is now preserved in the Windermere Steamboat Museum having lain at the bottom of the tarn for 35 years.

Although there are recorded well over 800 nursery rhymes in the *Oxford Nursery Rhyme Book*, surprisingly very few relate to angling. Most published collections of rhymes include Little Tommy Tittlemouse, who 'Lived in a little house', though there is occasional difference of opinion as to whether 'He caught fishes In other men's ditches', which is logical, or whether he caught them 'In other men's dishes', which isn't! The illustration is from a collection of *Favourite Nursery Rhymes* published by Blackie and Sons and illustrated by Frank Adams.

THE ANGLER'S FISH

British Fresh-water Fishes, one of the finest records of fish ever published in Britain, appeared in 1879. The author was a clergyman, the Rev. W. Houghton. The illustrator, Alexander Francis Lydon, was resident artist for some 30 years for the well-known lithographic printer Benjamin Fawcett. Fawcett had made a brilliant breakthrough in colour printing technique by engraving extremely fine lines on to Turkish box wood for the key and colour blocks. Up to seven separate sets were produced for individual pictures and printing was done only on hand presses. As a result the colours for each fish were reproduced with astonishing fidelity.

Subsequently the development of the copper printing plate and fast, accurate machine presses made it possible to print colour guides to fish in large quantities. But few, if any, have subsequently matched the gentle and sensitive textures of those achieved by Fawcett.

Three fish from the Rev. W. Houghton's *British Fresh-water Fishes*. BELOW: Salmon (male), RIGHT: Pike and TOP RIGHT: Bull Trout.

THE ANGLER'S GEAR

Angling gear, or so it appears, has altered little down the ages. The gentleman of 1647 pictured below, had he been attired for angling instead of simply walking out, would have looked little different to his counterpart of the 1930s, clad in Hardy's gear. Heavy boots and staff (or is it some form of ingenious telescopic rod?), waterproof cape and broad-brimmed hat perfectly attire this gent for the brotherhood of the angle – though like the Hardy-clad angler of three centuries later he may have had cause to regret quite so many buttons for his line to catch in.

Hardy Brothers thought of everything – or so it would seem. The bee-keeper's helmet aided by fumigation from the pipe, may have kept the cleggs at bay, but just try casting in that little lot. Better the 'Between' waders with zip fastener front designed 'to avoid that cupful of water which is occasionally shipped when using ordinary wading stockings!'

KEEPER OF THE STREAM

The keeper and the boatman both figure prominently in almost every angler's experience, sometimes too prominently for comfort. Indeed few sports have produced characters who were so frequently so much larger than life, or who had such capacity for the dram of whisky (or two or four).

'In Flagrante' by Charles Keen (1823-1891).
Keeper (coming on him unawares): 'Do you call this Fishing with a Fly, sir?'
Brigson: 'Eh? – I ah – well, I – Look here – have a – (diving for his flask) – take a nip? Do!!'
Reproduced from the *Punch Almanack*, 1885.

Rod Pole or Perch

'To fish, *fine, and far off* is the first and principal Rule for Trout Angling'. So wrote Charles Cotton in Part 2 of the *Compleat Angler*, 1676.

To achieve this, succeeding generations of anglers used rods of enormous length – and therefore great weight – in some cases exceeding 20 feet, well into the 19th century. Not surprisingly perhaps because Cotton himself had written of rods 'one of five or six yards is commonly enough, and larger . . . it ought not to be'. Although false-casting to dry the fly was not universal, and indeed was almost unknown at this time, great strength and stamina must nevertheless have been needed for a day of supposedly contemplative recreation wielding such a rod as this.

Even the early split cane rods were notable for their length and weight. As late as 1885, the distinguished angler Francis Francis was comparing the merits of four of his rods, all between 11 feet 6 inches and 12 feet 8 inches long and all weighing not far short of a pound, in the sixth edition of his *Book on Angling*. Indeed he clearly states his preference for double-handed rods of 14 feet or 14 feet 6 inches. Hardy's 'Connemara' salmon rod, advertised in their 1908 catalogue, was 16 feet long and weighed 28½ ounces.

It is to American influence that development of the lighter, shorter rod can be traced. The lightness and power of his 8 foot 2 inches American Leonard Rod was such a revelation to G.E.M. Skues that he called it the WBR – World's Best Rod.

One thing however is clear. Throughout the 19th century angling – in all its forms – and muscles, must have been synonymous.

Rods are not, in the main, widely collected. But an exception is the Grant Vibration Rod, made from greenheart by Alexander Grant, the Scot. With a 17-foot Vibration salmon rod, Grant made a tournament cast of 65 yards at Inverness in 1895 without shooting any line. When fishing, he is reported frequently to have hooked fish at a distance of 50 yards or more. Instead of ferrules, the Grant Vibration had spliced joints making for an exceptionally smooth and sweet action.

THE RISING GENERATION: ~ ~ THE SPORTSMAN.

JOHN HIGGINBOTHAM,

FISHING-ROD-MAKER,

At the GOLDEN FISH, No. 91,

opposite *Southampton-Street*, STRAND;

MAKES all Sorts of Fishing-Rods, and all Manner of the best Fishing Tackle, Wholesale and Retail, and sells the right KIRBY's and FORD's HOOKS, so much admired for their Goodness of Temper; with the best Sorts of Swivels, Winches, Artificial Flies, Mice, &c.

Minnow, Perch, and Jack Tackle fitted up in the neatest Manner.

Great Choice of curious White Silk Worm Gut, just come over.

The best Sorts of POWDER FLASKS, made in Metal, Tin, Leather, Horn, &c. to any Pattern or Size.—Magazines, Shot-Belts, Pouches, &c. &c.

Best Battel Gunpowder, Shot, and Flints of all Sorts.

*** TREATISES on ANGLING.

LEFT
This advertisement was pasted into a 1792 edition of Charles Bowlker's *The Art of Angling*.

BELOW
'The Fisherman'. An early 19th century steel engraving depicting an angler of impressive strength, to judge by the prodigious length of his rod.

ABOVE
Hardy Brothers made a miniature replica of a 'Palakona' split bamboo rod which they presented to Queen Mary for her Dolls' House in April 1924. The rod was in three pieces and when joined its length was 16 inches. The case in which the rod was housed measured, seven inches.

THE ANGLER'S CAST Alias Casting Around (or slinging the lead)

Theories of casting – more properly described as the art of propelling the fly, bait or lure to the fish – have been legion.

Nowhere has fly-casting been more elegantly illustrated than in Frederic M. Halford's *Dry Fly Fishing*, first published in 1889 (RIGHT). The angler's attire in particular is beyond reproach – not surprising as the 'model' was none other than the immortal George Selwyn Marryat. Since he is shown side view on – and his hands are not always visible – the illustrations are however of limited value as instruction.

BELOW

If an angler is requested by another angler, who is practising with a new casting reel, to retire, clear off, or sling his hook, he should sling it before the angler with the new reel does.

20

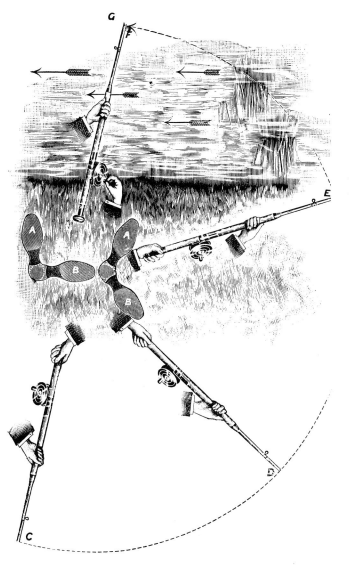

More practical perhaps than Frederic Halford's elegant illustration, although almost impossible to translate into action, are the instructions for bait-casting contained in Hardy Brothers catalogues over many years from 1898 showing how to use the patent 'Silex' reel. The commotion made on the bank by the inexperienced user of the reel must have frightened every fish for miles.

THE REEL THING

Fishing reels have latterly become items of great prize – and price – amongst collectors. Prices paid at auction for fishing reels have always considerably exceeded those generally fetched by rods and other items of tackle.

Very early examples exist of primitive line-winders made out of wood and bone. Brass however became the principal material from which reels came to be made in the late 18th century. Brass lent itself well to engraving and reels were often finely decorated and embellished as a result. Wood which could be quickly turned by lathe to form a drum and back plate largely replaced brass for general purpose fishing reels for some 80 years from around 1860. By the late 19th century, reels made from alloys were becoming commonplace, mostly for specialist purposes such as flyfishing, spinning or beach-casting. A noted example was Allcock's Aerial reel, precision engineered with particularly fine free running qualities. The first reel to use the face-forward principle, allowing the line to flow from the reel with minimum resistance, was made by Mallochs of Perth and patented in September 1884, to be followed by the Illingworth Threadline reel in 1905. Most prized by contemporary collectors are the reels made by Hardy Brothers of Alnwick, a range launched with the famous Perfect reel in 1891 and designed by Forster Hardy, the engineer of the family. Multiplying reels had been advertised since 1770 but only became commonplace in the 1920s, largely following designs patented in the USA by the famous makers Vom Hoff.

ABOVE
Three reels included in the Angler's Record issued by Ogden Smiths in the late 1930s. The 'Aerial' and 'Allcock Stanley' were both manufactured by S. Allcock and Co Ltd of Redditch. The 'British' was a fine centre pin reel turned out of walnut with a brass star back, flange and rim, with optional check.

ABOVE
A bronzed brass four-inch Malloch patent spinning reel with a reversible spool.

RIGHT
Illingworth No. 2 and No. 1 reels, illustrating the position for casting and taken from the original price list.

A selection of reels manufactured by Hardy Brothers and featured in their 1934 catalogue including the 'Super Silex' casting reel, the 'Perfect' fly reel, the 'Altex' fixed spool casting reel and Hardys 'Compensating' check mechanism.

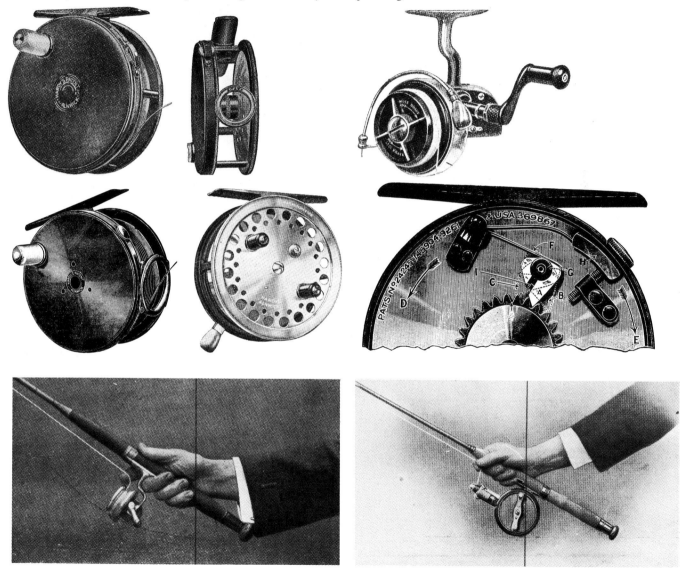

Hook Line and Sinker

Terminal tackle does not imply the equipment with which the angler finishes his fishing life – but what gets tied on to the reel line and beyond. It could in fact be described as the business end of the apparatus, and truthfully so because of its propensity to get lost should the hook snag in the bottom of the river, the opposite bank, or even more likely, a passing boat. The expectation of losing terminal tackle is such that almost every angler has at some time made it an excuse to stock up well, taking many more trips to the tackle shop than strictly necessary, greatly to the benefit of the trade.

Before the angler can hook a fish, he must himself be hooked by the fishing tackle manufacturer. One of the inducements of the trade is the brand names given to items of terminal tackle, lines in particular. The label for Ligne Samson, of French manufacture, depicts an angler attempting to pull Samson's hair out. Allcocks used 'Hercules' as a brand name for their casts or leaders. Ogden Smiths sold Magnet Hooks. And so it went on. All good fun and presumably, good business, too.

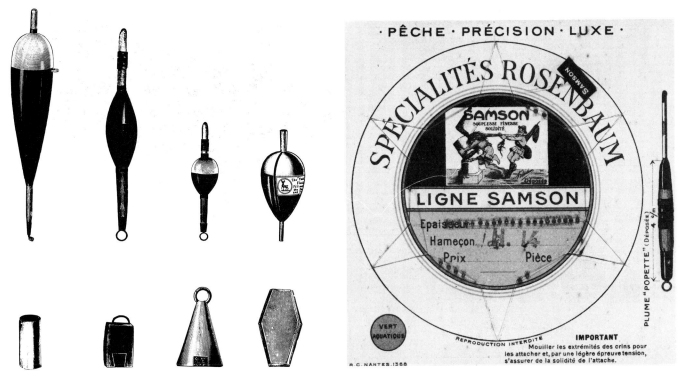

You see the ways the Fisherman doth take
To catch the fish: what engines doth he make?
Behold! how he engageth all his wits;
Also his snares, lines, angles, hooks and nets;
Yet fish there be, that neither hook nor line
Nor snare, nor net, nor engine can make thine;
They must be grop'd for, and be tickled too,
Or they will not be catch'd, whate'er you do.

John Bunyan
The Pilgrim's Progress

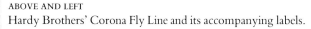

CARE OF WATERPROOF LINES
All oil dressed waterproof lines should be exposed to the air as much as possible. After use, they should be wound on to a line winder and carefully dried. If not required for some time, take them off the reels and hang up in an airy place.

HARDY BROS. (ALNWICK), LTD.,
ALNWICK, ENGLAND.

ABOVE AND LEFT
Hardy Brothers' Corona Fly Line and its accompanying labels.

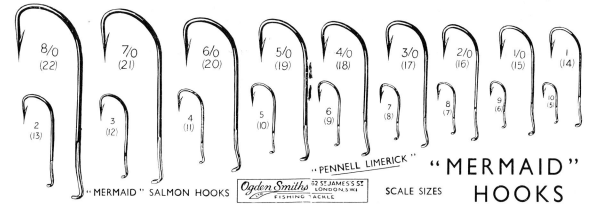

OGDEN SMITHS "MERMAID" DOUBLE HOOKS, BRAZED   OGDEN SMITHS "MERMAID" TREBLE HOOKS, BRAZED

"MERMAID" SALMON HOOKS   "PENNELL LIMERICK"   SCALE SIZES

Ogden Smiths 62 St JAMES'S S!
LONDON, S.W.1
FISHING TACKLE

"MERMAID" HOOKS

25

THE END OF THE LINE

At the end of the day, what really counts is what is tied on to the end of the line to deceive the wary fish. Over the years all manner of contraptions have been devised, most elegant among them the magnificent hand tied salmon flies. Originally such flies were tied with twisted gut eyes. However from the 1880s they were increasingly available on eyed hooks. None were finer than those sold by Hardys over the years and illustrated on the right, the majority of designs featuring as a 'cheek' a black and white feather from a pure bred jungle cock.

Perhaps nowhere however has more ingenuity been displayed than in the development of artificial spinning baits – which anti-kink devices notwithstanding have spun more fishermen's lines into impossible tangles than any sane fisher would care to think about.

The "Houghton" Eyed Fly and Cast Box

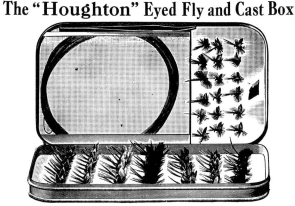

Made of **Japanned Tin,** with felt lining. Will hold 20 doz. eyed flies and one doz. gut casts. Size, $7 \times 3\frac{5}{8} \times \frac{7}{8}$ ins, - - Price **11/6**
With corrugated cork bars, instead of felt lining, - **16/6**
"Pennell" Fly Tweezers and Cutters, - - - **2/6 extra.**

Hardy's Fly Minnows
In colour, see Plate 19. Opp. page 236.

No. 1. **1/6** each.   No. 2. **2/3** each.

A most natural imitation of the minnow, and a capital bait for all predatory fish, especially in a brown water. They are fished in the same manner as a salmon fly. In the No. 2 size the spinner alone revolves and so advertises the lure. Dressed with extra strong hooks for Mahseer, 3d. each extra.

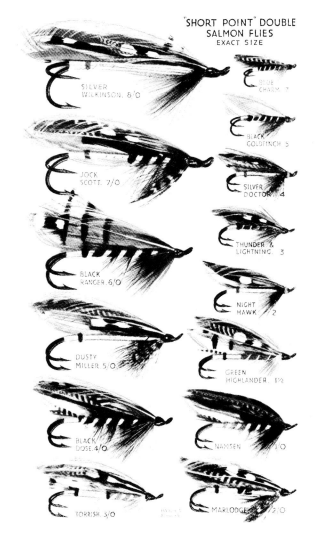

"SHORT POINT" DOUBLE SALMON FLIES
EXACT SIZE

SILVER WILKINSON. 6/0
BLUE CHARM. 7
JOCK SCOTT. 7/0
BLACK GOLDFINCH 5
SILVER DOCTOR. 4
BLACK RANGER. 6/0
THUNDER & LIGHTNING. 3
NIGHT HAWK 2
DUSTY MILLER 5/0
GREEN HIGHLANDER. 1½
BLACK DOSE. 4/0
NAMSEN 1/0
TORRISH. 3/0
MARLODGE 2/0

ADVERTISEMENTS ILLUSTRATED.

"*THE SCARER*.—THE MOST SPORTING AND DEADLY ARTIFICIAL MECHANICAL MINNOW NOW ON THE MARKET. FRIGHTENS THE FISH OUT OF THE WATER. WRITE FOR ONE NOW AND MAKE CERTAIN OF A GOOD BASKET. ONLY TWO-AND-SIXPENCE EACH. LARGER SIZE, TWICE AS DEADLY, FOUR-AND-SIXPENCE."

From *Punch*, 13 August 1919.

LEFT AND RIGHT

The 'Kill Devil' made by Foster Brothers of Ashbourne in Derbyshire. It had vanes at the back as well as the front better to disturb the water and 'thus tend to hide the nakedness of the hooks'.

RIGHT and BELOW

A selection of spinners, plugs and minnows from S. Allcock's *Angler's Guide* for 1938-9.

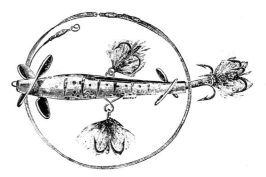

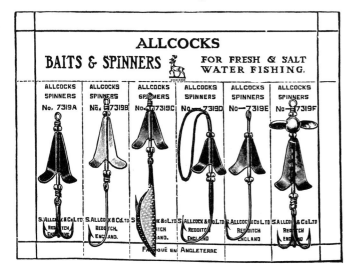

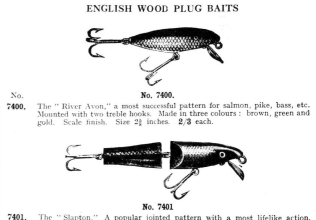

ENGLISH WOOD PLUG BAITS

No. 7400.

No.
7400. The "River Avon," a most successful pattern for salmon, pike, bass, etc. Mounted with two treble hooks. Made in three colours : brown, green and gold. Scale finish. Size 2⅝ inches. **2/3** each.

No. 7401

7401. The "Slapton." A popular jointed pattern with a most lifelike action. Mounting and colour as **7400.** Size 3½ inches. **3/-** each.

THE NATURAL TROUT FLY . . .

What delicacy of eye and touch are required perfectly to reproduce with silk, fur and feather the natural fly. *How* perfect that reproduction should be however has been, and still is, a matter for endless debate.

The exact imitation school would have anglers believe that the closer the artificial to the natural fly, the more readily the deception is likely to be made. Per contra, there are those who believe in impressionism, arguing that the natural can never be exactly reproduced and therefore that the artificial fly tied to give a general, impressionistic effect works better.

Whatever the adherents of Halford and exactitude – or their opponents – may say, trout, the final arbiters, will fall prey to flies tied either way.

Three stages in the development of the natural fly, in this case the mayfly (*Ephemera danica*) – nymph, subimago or dun and imago or spent fly, as illustrated in Halford's *Dry Fly Fishing in Theory and Practice*, together with his own artificial to represent the dun.

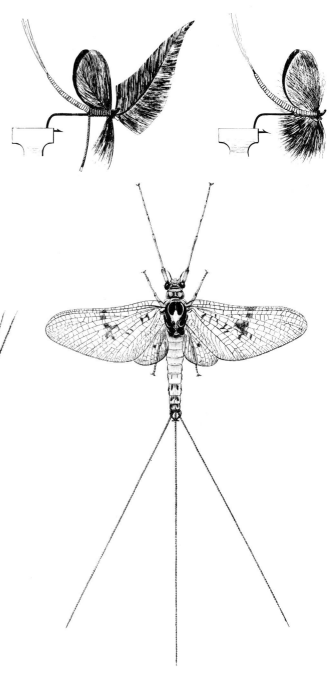

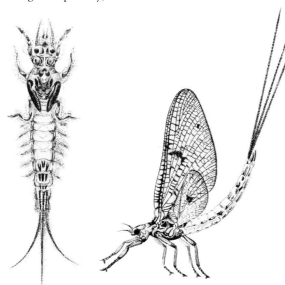

. . . And Its Imitation

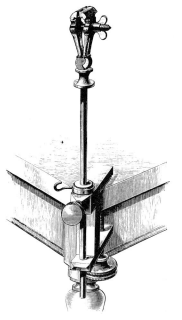

ABOVE
The 'Holtzapffel Fly-Dresser's Vice' used by Halford.

RIGHT
Some of Halford's patterns. What anticipation their very names conjure – Drake's Extractor, No. 1 Whitchurch, Hare's Ear Quill. And what of the India Rubber Olive, in use 100 years before the so-called 'new' latex flies of the 1980s.

ABOVE
Six stages in tying a dry fly, starting with the wings tied on to the hook shank and conclud-ing with the finished fly ready for its whip finish, as depicted in Halford's *Floating Flies and How to Dress Them*, 1886.

Detached Olive.

Nº 1 Whitchurch.

India Rubber Olive.

Dark Olive Quill

Medium Olive Quill

Pale Olive Quill.

Hare's Ear Quill

Drake's Extractor.

ALIVE ALIVE-O

Over the years the ubiquitous worm has proved the most popular of baits for fishing as cigarette cards in the Wills' series shown on this page clearly demonstrate. Indeed in this series, the lowly worm figures on almost half the cards which shows fish and the baits most commonly used to catch them.

The maggot, or gentle, must follow the worm in popularity, and indeed a substantial industry is now devoted to their breeding simply to satisfy the fishermens' needs.

Who indeed was the wag who said "You'll never crawl alone"? Incongruously it was George Kelson, author of the great book on salmon flies, who produced one of the strongest defences for the use of the worm. Writing in the *Fishing Gazette* on 17 January 1885 he said 'Unfortunately, we are brought up to believe that "worms", "kill-devils", and the like, are only fit for poachers and here I beg to differ once more from reputed authorities, for, in my opinion, a man is not a complete angler unless he understands all about the management of worms and other lures as well as flies'.

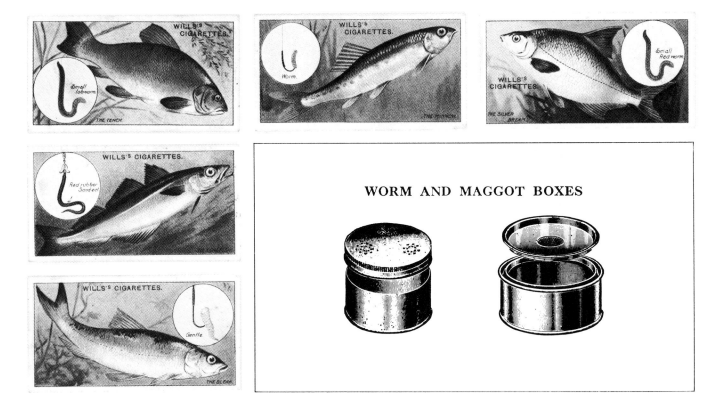

WORM AND MAGGOT BOXES

"LUVLY GRUB — LUVLY GRUB!"

If two members of a fly-fishing club are caught using natural bait, the gentleman with the larger worm should apologise first.

Happy Landings

God grant that I may love to fish
Until my dying day,
And when it comes to my last cast,
I'll then most humbly pray,
When in The Lord's safe landing net
I'm peacefully asleep,
That, in His mercy, I'll be judged
As good enough to keep.

Death is a fisherman – the world we see
A fish-pond is, and we the fishes be;
He sometimes angler-like doth with us play,
And slyly takes us one by one away.

Epitaph in High Wycombe Churchyard

Here lies poor Thompson all alone,
As dead and cold as any stone.
In wading in the river Nith,
He took a cold, which stopp'd his breath.
He fish'd the stream for ten years past,
Death caught him in his net at last.

Written on a tombstone in Dumfries,
1790

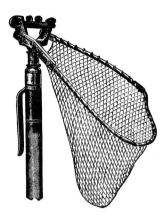

If the bending rod and the ringing reel
Give proof that you've fastened the tempered steel,
Be sure that the battle is but begun
And not till he's landed is victory won.

LEFT
'Trout – A Beauty'. Raphael Tuck postcard illustrated by A. Roland Knight.

Perhaps the supreme moment of suspense in angling is when the spent fish is at the angler's feet, ready to be drawn, deftly from the water.

Probably more tales of angling woe start from this point than any other.

Ultimate indignity – for the angler himself to have to be landed.

'Then the trout fell through a hole in my wretched net . . .'. One of C. F. Tunnicliffe's illustrations from *Going Fishing* by Negley Farson

THE ANGLER'S SOLACE

The flask frae my pocket
I poured into the socket,
For I was provokit unto the last degree;
And to my way o' thinkin',
There's naething for't but drinkin',
When a trout he lies winkin' and lauchin' at me.

W. C. Stewart

Hic jacet Walter Gun,
Very fond of angling fun;
Sic transit gloria mundi.
He drank hard upon Friday,
That being a high day,
Then took to his bed, and died upon Sunday.

LEFT
Donald McGill postcard. McGill, who was one of the most prolific illustrators of his day, is credited with over 9000 postcard designs.

The angler sits upon the bank
(For so the fish are cozened).
And drinks each time he gets a
                                    bite
And each time when he doesn't

It's nice to sit and think and fish,
And fish and sit and think,
And think and fish and sit and wish
That you could get a drink.

LEFT
It must be distinctly understood that the custom of drinking 'Good Luck' after landing a fish applies to salmon only and *not* to roach.

In The Bag

The skill of the angler can be judged by the weight of his creel – or so it used to be said. How much more elegant was this carrier, RIGHT, made of finest English willow, than the plastic bag which has so widely replaced it today.

This print demonstrates how the elegant angler of the early 1800s wore his creel.

Two creels from Hardy Brothers' catalogue of 1936. The 'Houghton' was specially designed for the dry-fly angler to carry three brace of Test trout in two separate compartments.

The Angler's Accessories

Anglers' accessories appearing in Hardy's Catalogue for 1936. 1. The 'Allinone' Fly Fisher's Case, divided into compartments to hold an Aluminium fly hook, a chamois leather and parchment three-pocket cast case and a cast damper with felt pads. On the cover is a pocket to hold a sportsman's balance. 2. The 'Carry All' Case. 3. The 'Tweed' salmon fisher's cast case made of crocodile calf leather 'in very superior style'. 4. The 'Onview' fly book and mounted cast case with pigskin cover. 5. The 'Glencoe' mounted cast case of Japanned tin so constructed that 'casts and flies cannot possibly entangle'. 6. The 'Houghton' trout fisher's cast case of which Hardy wrote 'We need hardly remind anglers that chamois is the very best of all materials to protect gut in any climate'

RIGHT
Accessories listed in S. Allcock's catalogue for 1936.

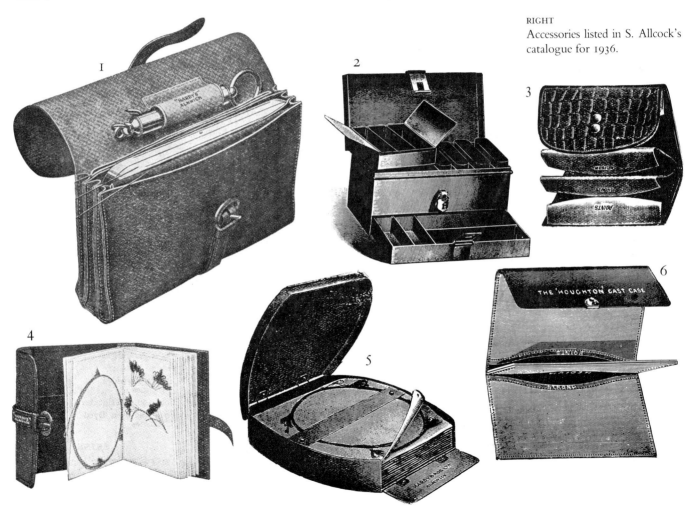

ALLCOCKS
REDDITCH

FISH RULE, BALANCES, Etc.

No. 9028

No.
9028. Aluminium Fish Rule, 14 inches long (open), showing minimum lengths of fish which may be retained in the Severn Fishery District. **1/3** each.

No. 0522

0522. Brass Balance by 1 oz. to 3 lbs., **6/9**; 1 oz. to 4 lbs., **7/6** each.
522a. Brass Balance by ¼ lb. to :

	6	10	15	20	lbs.
	5/-	6/6	7/6	11/9	each.

522. Brass Balance by ½ lb. to :

	7	12	20	30	50	lbs.
	5/-	5/-	6/6	7/6	15/-	each.

WIRE CUTTING SCISSORS *(Foreign)*

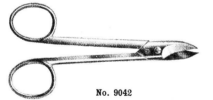

No. 9042

9042. A most useful article for those anglers who prefer to make up their own wire traces. Length 4½ inches. **3/-** each.

No. 4820

4820. The "Alpha," nickelled and folding. An old favourite. Length open, 3¾ inches. **4d.** each.

No. 8899

8899. "Selecta" Paste. Few baits are more killing for roach than bread paste. That it is not more largely used is due entirely to the trouble entailed in preparing it and to the fact that fresh supplies must be made up for each outing. All this has been done away with by the new method of packing it in sealed tubes all ready for use. One tube will last most anglers for a whole season. It is particularly economical, for only sufficient paste to cover the hook is squeezed out when required. There is no waste, no mess and the paste is always clean and fresh. **10d.** per tube.

FLY VICE, TWEEZERS AND PLIERS

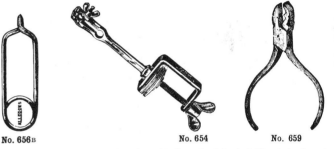

No. 656B   No. 654   No. 659

654. Small nickelled Fly-tying Vice, with clamp for fixing to table. A simple and popular pattern. **9/-** each.
656B. Fly Tweezers, nickelled steel. **1/-** pair.
659. Shot Cutter and Pliers combined. **1/6** each.

DISGORGERS, Etc.—contd.

No. 8894

No.
8894. The "O.K." disgorger. A simple disgorger certain in its action. Hollowed and split at the end, the disgorger follows easily down the gut and grips the hook firmly. Made of bright aluminium. 6 inches long. **6d.** each.

Open   No. 6212   Closed

6212. The "Gripwell," nickelled and folding. Length open, 4 inches. **7d.** each.

37

THE ANGLER'S ACCESSORIES

Hardy Brothers of Alnwick have always produced a fine range of angler's sundries and accessories. All were made with the precision and durability associated with Hardy products which guaranteed that they would last well. Many have survived as a result to become collectors' items today and are even more valuable if they have been preserved in their original boxes. All the items on these pages come from Hardy's *Angler's Guides* for 1934 and 1937.

THE " CURATE " (Regd. 557672.)

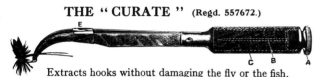

Extracts hooks without damaging the fly or the fish.

A combination of the following useful anglers' tools.—Small Priest ; Tweezers, or a disgorger ; Gut Cutter E ; Reservoir **C,** to hold oil for reels ; Stiletto **B,** to apply oil or clean the eye of a hook. The handle may be used as a match striker. Price **5/6** each.

No. 2.

As an all-round Angler's Knife, this is a very useful pattern. It comprises the following Tools :

LARGE BLADE.
SCISSORS.
CORKSCREW.
STILETTO.
SCREW-DRIVER.

Fitted with Stout Shackle (at opposite end to that shown) to which a Chain may be attached. Suitable Chains with Spring Clip 2/6 each.

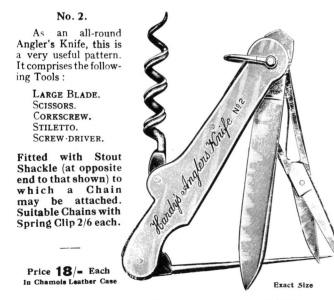

Price **18/-** Each
In Chamois Leather Case

Exact Size

Made in Sterling Silver at proportionate prices.

The Scissor Plier

An entirely new and most interesting tool.

The tool comprises a pair of strong snipping scissors furnished at the ends of the blades with a small plier grip. The dual purpose of the tool is called for during the same operation, i.e. tying a fly to the cast or a knot in gut or subdugut. Before cutting off the surplus ends the knots are pulled tight by the pliers. Greater power is obtained when using the pliers if the middle finger is hooked into the loop of one handle while the palm grips the other.

The scissor blades are serrated to hold and cut stiff gut easily.

Price **4/-** each.

TWEEZERS, GUT CUTTER AND DISGORGER

A useful article for cutting off gut ends, or extracting flies from the box or fish. The handle end is formed as a disgorger and turn screw. Illustration is actual size. Price **2/6** each.

The " Wethered " Net Carrier

A handy little clip which may be placed on the creel strap, and will carry net or gaff by pushing the handle through the clip. To remove, the handle is simply forced out. Price, **1/-** each.

Fly Makers' Vices

THE "HARDY-COULIN"
Suitable for Small Flies

In designing this vice we have been kindly assisted by Mons. E. Coulin, an ardent amateur fly dresser.

The vice and locking ring being perfectly plain there is no liability of the tying silk, etc., becoming entangled with parts of the vice whilst working. The work is held at an angle which permits both hands to operate with ease. Fitted with adjustable table clamp. Price 9/- each.

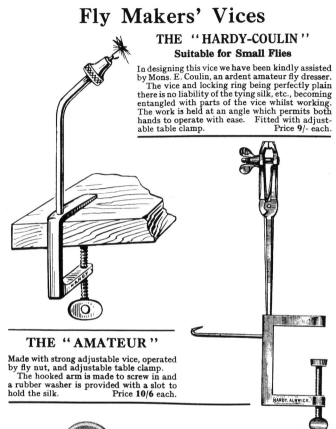

THE "AMATEUR"

Made with strong adjustable vice, operated by fly nut, and adjustable table clamp.

The hooked arm is made to screw in and a rubber washer is provided with a slot to hold the silk. Price 10/6 each.

WAISTCOAT POCKET FLY OIL BOTTLE

A convenient form for the waistcoat pocket. The interior is fitted with a long sleeve, which prevents the oil flowing back when filled to line mark. PRICE 3/6 each.

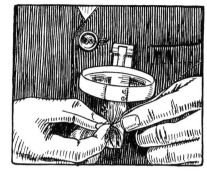

The "WARDLE" MAGNIFIER
Regd. No. 704251

We are indebted to Major Wardle for this excellent idea. The magnifier is carried by a safety pin fastening to the coat and is always handy for immediate use. When not in use it closes up against the body quite out of the way.

Price 10/6 each.

Hardy's Clearing Knife

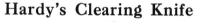

Made of Steel, Silver Plated, and fitted in Pigskin Pocket. 5/- each.

Rod Rest for Trolling or Sea Fishing

The socket and spindle with pinching screw permits the direction of the rod to be altered, while the arms are so arranged that the angle of the rod can be adjusted as desired. Price, 15/6 each.

FISHING TYPES

Wherever there is water, men (and boys) will fish, crudely designated Game, Coarse or Sea anglers depending on the nature of the quarry and their habitat. These appellations are misleading. Skilled roach fishers or pike addicts will reject the 'coarse' designation with as much justification as the angler in pursuit of seatrout off the shores of The Hebrides repudiates any suggestion that he is a sea angler. Indeed within these classifications there is room for even further dispute. Can the worm-fisher for salmon really warrant the title of game fisher? What is the difference between spinning for salmon and spinning for mackerel?

LEFT
Dry Fly Fishing. The delicacy of the dry fly angler is captured perfectly in this 1923 pen drawing by Lionel Edwards.

ALL AT SEA

The Sea Angler

There was a gentle angler who was angling in the sea,
With heart as cool as only heart, untaught of love, can be;
When suddenly the waters rushed, and swelled, and up there sprung
A humid maid of beauty's mould – and thus to him she sung:

'Why dost thou strive so artfully to lure my brood away,
And leave them then to die beneath the sun's all-scorching ray?
Couldst thou but tell how happy are the fish that swim below,
Thou wouldst with me, and taste of joy which earth can never
know.

'Does not bright Sol – Diana too – more lovely far appear
When they have dipped in ocean's wave their golden, silvery hair?
And is there no attraction in this heaven-expanse of blue,
Nor in thine image mirrored in this everlasting dew?'

The water rushed, the water swelled, and touched his naked feet,
And fancy whispered to his heart it was a love-pledge sweet:
She sung another siren lay, more 'witching than before,
Half-pulled – half plunging – down he sunk, and ne'er was heard of
more.

Goethe

RIGHT
'Surf-casting is not a duffer's sport.' A fine illustration by C. F.
Tunnicliffe from Negley Farson's *Going Fishing*

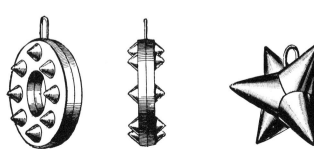

THE FISHING TACKLE SHOP

Where would the angler be without the tackle shop?

Expeditions have to be made, frequently, to this Mecca. Indeed the anticipation of such a visit is matched only by the prospect of fishing itself.

Whatever the declared objective, deep down the true angler will nurse the hope of finding some irresistible lure or a line which will cast just that bit further to previously unreachable fish. Permutations of expectations are endless.

Then there is the assistant. Anyone who has ever stood for any length of time in a tackle shop will know that triumphs or disasters have to recounted – and are. If patience is essential for the angler, it is doubly so for the tackle shop assistant, though for reasons quite different.

Most embellished of all British tackle shops until the early 1950s was Ogden Smith's premises in St James's Street, London (BELOW LEFT). The fascia of the shop was green and adorned across its front were two magnificent hooks, painted in gold.

John Cheek, whose stock was catholic, had premises at 52 Strand, London, when he issued the catalogue illustrated (BELOW RIGHT) in 1844. Around 1850 he opened a shop at 132c Oxford Street. Cheek set great store by having good neighbours. The Strand shop was billed as 'Opposite the British Fire Office'. The Oxford Street premises advertised as 'Between Holles Street, and Old Cavendish Street, Directly opposite Royal College of Chemistry'.

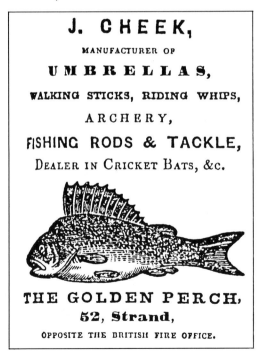

THE FISHING TACKLE CATALOGUE

If the angler is not fishing what better than to be ensconced in a large armchair, with a large whisky and a fishing tackle catalogue.

Heavily illustrated catalogues have been a feature of the angler's world since the 1880s. As well as listing tackle and equipment, many have contained general articles ranging from angling technique to where to fish.

Hardy Brothers of Alnwick regularly produced one of the most comprehensive guides to game-fishing tackle (BELOW LEFT). In addition to their game-fishing catalogue Hardys also advertised a catalogue, in a less promiscuous age, for 'Bottom' or 'Still' fishing named 'Hardy's Super Bottom Fishing Tackle'.

Ogden Smith, Farlow (BELOW RIGHT), Malloch of Perth, Cummins of Bishop Auckland and many others issued catalogues to the angling public. Catalogues were also issued to the trade only by such manufacturers as S. Allcock of Redditch and stores like the Army & Navy in London.

Old catalogues are now widely sought after by collectors and have become the major source of identifying tackle.

POACHED SALMON

There are many tales of poaching in angling literature, one of the most gripping and memorable being in Buchan's *John MacNab* (1925). But this invests the poacher with a glamour which is not properly his due.

A notable exception is *The Confessions of a Poacher*, edited by John Watson F.L.S. Published in 1890, the book recounts the memories of 80-year-old 'Phil', an incorrigible poacher. Villain he may have been but Watson gives him the accolades of sportsman and naturalist – as the professional 19th-century poacher probably had to be to survive.

ABOVE
Dragging a deep 'dub' with a long net.

ABOVE
'The charges: trespassing, night poaching, being in possession of illegal fish, illegally taking salmon and with being in possession of 129 salmon and trout during the close season.'

RIGHT
'In thanking us for a silvery five-pound salmon we gave him he spoke with a southern accent . . .'

Fortunate the angler whose interests embrace the natural world around him. How often has a day been made for the solitary angler by the emerald flash of the kingfisher – or even more rarely by one actually alighting on his rod. What of the heron, disturbed from the water's edge, leaping, awkwardly, skywards? Poachers extraordinary – along with the osprey and the cormorant.

The most famous illustrator of birds in Victorian Britain was John Gould. Between 1862 and 1873 he issued five separate volumes in which were magnificently illustrated the country's native birds, providing the most comprehensive contemporary record of birds and their habitats. Plates from the original printing are now collectors' items.

One of Gould's favourite haunts for observing birds was on the banks of the River Thames at Taplow. He frequently travelled the 25 miles from London to watch river life and fish there, his only recreation. This probably helps explain not only why his water birds were so exactly executed, but why their habitats were so faithfully depicted too.

RIGHT
Osprey. An adult bird with prey (lake trout) which it catches lengthwise, holding the fish with one claw in front of the other. John Gould 1870

THE ANGLER'S MISHAPS

To be chased by a bull, to fall in, to sit on a wasp's nest or to hook the boatman firmly in his ear, are all common hazards of angling. Indeed fishing is so fraught that the outsider might wonder why any sane person should ever attempt it.

Two plates entitled, 'Some Mishaps in the Pleasures of Angling', illustrated by Charles Turner, are included here; they are from a set of six aquatints entitled 'The Delights of Fishing'. They were produced from watercolours by the early 19th-century amateur sporting artist Sir William Frankland (1784-1849). Sir William was obviously familiar with fishing disasters and included in his piece an angler slipping on a muddy bank, falling on and breaking his rod while the line parts, leaving his catch to go free. Meantime an angler in the background break his punt pole and is about to take the inevitable ducking.

In another print from the same series an angler pursued by a swarm of flies, is in turn about to be bitten by a dog which itself is being chased by a bull. Even greater disaster has struck the angling party caught by the bargee's tow rope. No 9 in the series 'Spooner's Magic' (RIGHT) records a mishap which many later illustrators were to copy.

FAR LEFT
Taking a fly. An aquatint usually attributed to Edward Rapnard of the Houghton Fishing Club. He died on 13 December 1801, in his 76th year.

LEFT
One of the lesser joys of angling. From an aquatint by Sir Robert Frankland.

LEFT
'Some Mishaps in the Pleasures of Angling'. Another aquatint engraved by Charles Turner after Sir Robert Frankland of Thirkleby Hall, near Thirsk.

BELOW
'Got a bite'. What a bite indeed! Late 19th-century steel engraving.

The Angler's Mishaps

FREAKS OF FANCY!

A BAIT.

Within the streams, Pausanias saith,
That down Cocytus valley flow,
Girdling the grey domain of Death,
The spectral fishes come and go,
The ghosts of fish flit to and fro.
Persephone, fulfil my wish
And grant that in the shades below
My ghost may land the ghosts of fish.

Andrew Lang
Grass of Parnassus

Why fliest thou away with fear?
Trust me there's naught of danger here;
I have no wicked hook,
All covered with a snaring bait,
Alas! to tempt thee to thy fate,
And drag thee from the brook.

Oh harmless tenant of the flood,
I do not wish to spill thy blood;
For nature unto thee
Perchance has given a tender wife
And children dear to charm thy life;
As she hath done to me.

Enjoy thy stream, oh harmless fish,
And when an angler for his dish,
Through gluttony's vile sin,
Attempts – a wretch – to pull thee out,
God give thee strength, oh gentle trout,
To pull the rascal in.

Dr John Wolcot

LEFT
'Freaks of Fancy', a series of prints of which this is No 8 published by S. Gans of Southampton Street, Strand in 1830. The caption reads 'A BAIT. Lawk how I should like to catch a Gudgeon'.

From 'The Spodnoodle Papers', 1923, by W. Heath Robinson which first appeared in *The Daily News.*

If an angler who is not an enthusiast suddenly wakes up, he should·first ascertain how his companions are getting on before enquiring if there is any more beer.

What angler has not dreaded the awesome prospect of an eel in his boat, a predicament clearly familiar to Thomas Bewick, the great English engraver, to whom this print has been attributed.

'The Gouty Angler' by Theodore Lane, one of the great fishing pictures, the original of which is now in the Tate Gallery, London. It has been reproduced in almost every conceivable way including, as here, a print. It was also a very popular subject on Victorian ceramic pot lids and later for postcards.

The Angler's Mishaps

The popularity of the coloured postcard in the early 20th century provided artists and illustrators with endless opportunities for humour at the angler's expense. Many different series were produced by postcard manufacturers – one of the most unusual being a series of cricketing phrases, which actually illustrated terms used in angling.

All the old 'saws' are to be found – the angler hooking himself, or the bank, or his companion; the angler chased by a bull, or having a dog eat his dinner, or steal his catch; the angler who falls in, gets soaked in a downpour, or frozen stiff; or the angler who loses his 'jar', popularly – and probably rightly – believed to be the main incentive to most of the fraternity to go fishing!

ABOVE

'Caught' – number 6 in a series of six cards (No 2541) 'Fishing Phrases', illustrated by Tom Browne, published by Davidson Brothers.

LEFT

'Humours of Fishing', illustrated by Charles Crombie, was published by the famous firm of Valentines.

ABOVE
Two cards issued by the German firm Ernest Nister of Nuremburg who were particularly noted for their ingenious 'moveable' picture books for children.

RIGHT
Another Tom Browne postcard, Number 3 in series 2507, 'Illustrated Sports', published by Davidson Brothers.

THE ANGLER AFLOAT

Since time immemorial, man has taken to the water to fish – whether Beatrix Potter's Jeremy Fisher on his lilypad or Beatrix's husband, William Hellis in his rickety fishing punt, in the tarn above their Cumberland home.

Boats were invariably well fitted out including in their accoutrements comfortable chairs for the angler to recline at ease.

Where punts were used, fishing pitches were frequently staked out with two poles to which the boat could be tethered across the stream.

Artists, being of vivid imagination, have often had strange ideas about the balancing capability of boats – and even stranger ideas about their carrying capacity.

BELOW

Fashionable angling from a punt. Drawn and engraved by Robert Pollard (1755-1838). Interestingly this print was signed by Pollard on the upper propelling pole. It was one of a series of four engravings illustrating elegant anglers' attire.

Fishing often featured in 19th-century political cartoons. Under the heading 'Angling Extraordinary', the Duke of Wellington says to Sir Robert Peel: 'When you rise a heavy fish, strike rather gently: give him plenty of line, and when you begin to wind up, do so quickly.' The politician was Morgan O'Connell and the artist John Doyle (1797-1868).

'Fishing in a punt'. From an aquatint in colour by J. Clark after a watercolour by Henry Alken (1785-1841), for the folio edition of Alken's *British Sports* published by Thomas McLean on 1 January 1820. Two other prints complete this set, 'Salmon Fishing' and 'Pike Fishing'.

'Punt Fishing'. From a 19th-century engraving by W. Burraud deftly drawing the social distinction between the gentleman seated in a chair, while his servant is left to sit astride the thwart.

THE ANGLER AFLOAT

LEFT
'A Member of A Thames Angling Club' from an engraving by W. B. Gardner published in the *Illustrated London News*, 6 September 1873.

Correct etiquette observed. One angler in this late 18th-century print waits while his companion lands his catch before re-casting.

ABOVE

'A snug angling party'. By Thomas Rowlandson, the famous early 19th-century artist and illustrator.

RIGHT

'River Humour; A Band of Hope', from series no 9233 published by Raphael Tuck & Sons, illustrated by Lance Thackeray who produced some 800 postcard designs of which 15 had angling themes. Thackeray used the technique of a 'follow-up' drawing at the side of the card on many of his designs, invariably adding thereby a humorous twist. Tucks designated these cards 'Oilette' Remarque (Illustrated Marginal Notes).

RIVER HUMOUR
A Band of Hope.

THE ANGLER'S MUSIC

The most celebrated piece of angler's music must be Franz Schubert's Quintet in A Major opus 114 for piano and strings, 'The Trout', which was written in 1819 when the composer was 22. The work owes its nickname to Schubert's song 'Die Forelle' which he used, slightly altered, as the theme for a set of variations in the fourth movement. The extent to which Schubert was influenced by watching trout in the Alpine streams around the village of Steyr in upper Austria is in some doubt, but it is known that he was extremely happy there for, in a letter to his brother Ferdanent, he wrote 'there are eight girls in the house I am living in and almost all of them are pretty'.

Perhaps stronger claims could be advanced for pride of place in the angler's music for Walton's 'Angler's Song', which has many times been set to music. But for clarity and vibrancy, so perfectly in tune with the movement of the active trout on a clear spring morning in a mountain stream, Schubert's piece must surely take the palm.

THE ANGLER'S DINNER

THE ANGLER'S WEATHER

There are those who doubt whether fisherman ever actually do catch fish. It is invariably too hot, or the wind is in the wrong direction, or there is too much, or not enough, rain . . . the excuses flow forth like the river itself in a seemingly never-ending torrent. Show me the angler who has never blamed one such as above and there indeed is an honest man or woman. The sad thing is that the angler's excuses are all too often true. But then there would not be all that much fun in fishing if big baskets were always guaranteed, as Mr Theodore Castwell, according to the story told by G. E. M. Skues, found to his cost on entering the Pearly Gates.

When the wind is in the east,
Tis neither good for man nor beast;
When the wind is in the north,
The skilful fisher goes not forth;
When the wind is in the south,
It blows the bait in the fishes' mouth;
When the wind is in the west,
Then 'tis at the very best.

O blessed drums of Aldershot!
O blessed south-west train!
O blessed, blessed Speaker's clock,
All prophesying rain!

O blessed yaffil, laughing loud!
O blessed falling glass!
O blessed fan of cold gray cloud!
O blessed smelling grass!

O bless'd south wind that toots his horn
Through every hole and crack!
I'm off at eight tomorrow morn,
To bring such fishes back!

                    Charles Kingsley
                    The South Wind

Dirty days hath September
April, June and November.
From January up till May,
The rain it raineth every day.
All the rest have thirty-one
Without a blessed gleam o'sun
And if any of them had two and thirty
They'd be just as wet – tho' twice as dirty.

Weathervanes are an important source of intelligence for the angler. Vanes incorporating fish are quite uncommon but amongst notable examples is that atop the church spire at Piddinghoe in Sussex from which a mullet loftily surveys a bend in the Ouse below. Another fine fish vane, this time a salmon, is sited on top of the Parish Church at Wareham on the Dorset Stour.

On the Pier

The Pleasures of Hope

LEFT
Angling like matrimony has often been described as the triumph of hope over experience.

THE ANGLER'S EXCUSES

Sometimes over early,
Sometimes over late,
Sometimes nae water,
Sometimes a spate,
Sometimes over calm,
Sometimes over clear,
There's aye something wrang,
When I'm fishing here.

Fishing, if I, a fisher may protest,
Of pleasures is the sweet'st, of sports the best,
Of exercises the most excellent;
Of recreations the most innocent.
But now the sport is marde, and wott ye why
Fishes decrease, and fishers multiply.

Thomas Bastard (1598)

We did not think it trouble
To watch each whirl and bubble;
We sought the brook, each shady nook,
And cast our fly and hook;
The day was dark and dreary,
We returned both wet and weary,
With broken rod and tangled line,
And called the fishing fine.

LEFT
'Hope. Well, I hope's I shall ketch something
soon. I've been here six-hours and not had a
bite yet!!!' Early proof that fish like the rain
even less than fishermen, contrary to all
popular belief.

THE GREAT ANGLERS

Who were the great anglers? Men like Nelson, who, when he lost his right arm, continued to fish with his left? Or are the great anglers the many, many folk who have been able over the years, regularly to catch large bags of large fish – but who have gone unrecorded for posterity? In truth those to whom this designation is usually now accorded are almost all people who wrote. Pride of place amongst anglers must go to old Izaak Walton, father of

modern angling, with his *Compleat Angler* in 1653, aided and abetted by Charles Cotton, whose second part of that masterly work appeared in 1676. But the names which have come down the years are those of the great 19th-century anglers whose writings have so influenced angling into the present day.

The Scottish writer W. C. Stewart, whose *Practical Angler* first

appeared in 1857, gave shrewd guidance on tactics and techniques to generations to come; Canon Greenwell, who achieved immortality with the Greenwell's Glory, universally effective as a wet or as a dry fly; William Scrope whose *Days and Nights of Salmon Fishing on the Tweed* published in 1843 broke little new ground for the salmon fisher but is a marvellous 'read'; Francis Francis, one of the amazing Victorian all-rounders whose *Book on Angling* (1865) was the fruit of an almost unrivalled experience gained during a lifetime of freshwater fishing or the peripatetic Augustus Grimble who charted the salmon rivers of England, Scotland and Ireland to the benefit of travelling anglers. Later Col. E. W. Harding produced a most valuable study on trout vision, underrated then as now, *The Fly Fisher & the Trout's Point of View* (1931) and in 1924 J. W. Dunne's *Sunshine and the Dry Fly* proposed how to emulate the translucent effects of light on the natural fly's body.

But dwarfing these and others including such legendary figures as Viscount Grey were two towering characters: Frederic M. Halford (PICTURED BELOW) and George Edward Mackenzie Skues.

The invention of the oiled-silk line had made upstream dry fly fishing much easier and had largely driven the wet fly from the south country chalk streams. Halford, and those close to him, determined to ensure the sovereignty of the dry fly. In all he produced seven books to reinforce his arguments beginning with *Floating Flies and How to Dress Them* in 1886 and concluding with the *Dry-Fly Man's Handbook* in 1913.

FAR LEFT
Izaak Walton as portrayed in John Major's edition of *The Compleat Angler* in 1823.

LEFT
Izaak Walton's premises near the corner of Chancery Lane, London EC4 also from John Major's 1823 edition of *The Compleat Angler*.

THE GREAT ANGLERS

Halford's theories were strongly challenged by George Edward Mackenzie Skues, RIGHT, sometime Winchester Scholar, bachelor, solicitor and lifelong member of the Flyfishers' Club. Convinced of the logic that trout clearly feeding underwater should be fished for underwater, Skues first advanced his theories – and practices – in his book *Minor Tactics of the Chalk Stream*, published in 1910.

Perhaps because the arguments were largely emotive, the dry fly purists and the nymph fishers locked in combat – a farce which still continues to be played out even to this day.

The sequel for Skues was tragic. Having fished his beloved Abbots Barton stretch of the River Itchen for over half a century, Skues left the syndicate which rented it because of controversy amongst his fellow members over his use of the tactics he had so strongly championed throughout a uniquely productive fishing life.

His wit is well exemplified by the verse below (parody of A. A. Milne though it is) which first appeared in the *Journal* of the Flyfishers' Club in 1925.

Nine Little Troutses

Once upon a time there were nine little troutses,
They hadn't no tails and they hadn't no snoutses;
They hadn't no fins and they hadn't no gillses,
For they'd put all these articles up the spoutses.

They swallowed no nymphs and they gulped no flieses,
They lay quite still and they made no rises;
They spent all their time on their little flat sideses,
And the spots which they hadn't were of different sizes.

They hadn't no yellow upon active flankses,
They jumped no jumpses and they played no prankses;
They chased no minnows and no sticklebackses,
And they none of them lay under sedge-hung bankses.

And in case my reader entertains some doubtses
If there ever were nine such peculiar troutses,
The reason they hadn't any gills or finses,
They'd been cooked and soldered up in air-tight tinses.

THE LADY ANGLER

Women figure little in the art or literature of angling from the late 19th century on. Two charming exceptions are included here. The picture below, which was reproduced in Walter Shaw Sparrow's *Angling in British Art*, was also used as the frontispiece to *Angling and Art in Scotland*, written and illustrated by Ernest Briggs R.I. (1866-1913). It was captioned 'The Gentle Art'.

Another exception is the series of postcards issued by Raphael Tuck & Sons and entitled 'The Lady Angler – The Day's Catch', and 'Playing her Fish' (RIGHT). A third card in the series was captioned 'A Rise'.

THE ANGLER'S DIARY

Upon a river's bank serene
A fisher sat, where all was green.
            And looked it.
He saw, when light was getting dim,
A fish, or else the fish saw him
            And hooked it.
He took, with high erected comb,
The fish, or else the tale home,
            And cooked it.
Recording angels round his bed.
Heard all that he had done – or said –
            And booked it.

The Fisherman's Prayer.

Lord, grant that I may catch a
            fish
So large that even I,
When telling of it afterwards,
May have no need to lie.

ABOVE
Budding diarists . . .

BELOW
The author's first fishing diary.

The angler who has never kept a diary is clearly the poorer for it, even if it has meant recourse to the device ascribed to a young man of his acquaintance by Montmorency in *Three Men in a Boat*.

He was a most conscientious fellow, and, when he took to fly-fishing, he determined never to exaggerate his hauls by more than twenty-five per cent.

'When I have caught forty fish,' said he, 'then I will tell people that I have caught fifty, and so on. But I will not lie any more than that, because it is sinful to lie.'

But the twenty-five per cent plan did not work well at all. He never was able to use it. The greatest number of fish he ever caught in one day was three, and you can't add twenty-five per cent to three – at least, not in fish.

So he increased his percentage to thirty-three-and-a-third, but that, again was awkward, when he had only caught one or two . . .

THE ANGLER'S JOURNAL

'Every Tuesday morning I am all impatience to get my favourite reading, *The Fishing Gazette*, to learn what there is new about angling matters. So it was on Tuesday 23rd December, when between 8 and 9 o'clock, the postman came and delivered to me your capital double illustrated winter number, which, just now, as the weather is so bad and wild, that one would hesitate to put a dog out of doors, afforded me a most agreeable pastime during the Christmas time.'

Could any publisher ask for a better testimonial than this, written to the editor of *The Fishing Gazette* by an Austrian subscriber Enid Weeger exactly 100 years ago? Probably the best known angling periodical ever, it passed into the hands of R. B. Marston in 1879, continuing under his editorship until his death 48 years later on 2 September 1927. It was much lamented in its eventual passing.

A COUNTRY LIFE PUBLICATION

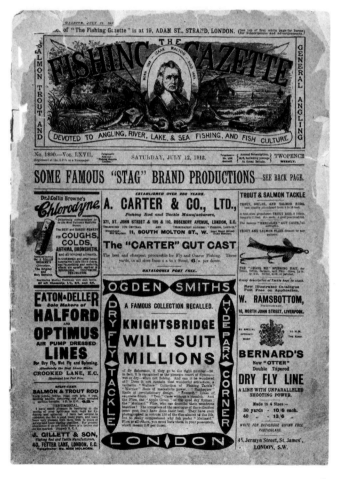

The Field or Country Gentleman's Newspaper was first published by Messrs Bradbury & Evans on 1 January 1853. The roll of its angling editors is daunting. The first was Francis Francis (1856-1883). He was succeeded by William Senior (1884-1900). C.H. Cook, who wrote under the nom-de-plume of John Bickerdyke, then held the angling editorship briefly (1900-1903); followed by the legendary H. T. Sheringham (1903-1930).

The Shooting Times, which has always devoted space to angling, was first published in 1882. The *Salmon and Trout Magazine* however is arguably now the oldest magazine to be published continuously for fishermen, having first been published in 1903.

THE ANGLER'S LIBRARY

How to build an angling library? That is the question. Should it be based on a few relative rarities like one of the 12 large paper copies of George Bainbridge's *The Fly-fishers Guide* (1816) or perhaps William Baigent's masterly book on hackles of which only some 65 copies were ever produced? Or should it be built on more catholic (and less expensive) lines? Whatever the basis, there are some 20 *musts*.

Pride of place for one of the most marvellous 'reads' in the literature of angling must go to Negley Farson's *Going Fishing*, first published in 1942. Farson, a master story-teller, was an overseas newspaper correspondent who fished all over the world whenever opportunity arose – and wrote about it with style and elegance. A similarly gentle book, which came unusually from the pen of a professional singer who was also an angler, is Harry Plunkett Greene's *Where the Bright Waters Meet* (1924), a tale of the tragic decline – and recreation – of a tiny Dorsetshire chalk stream. Do not be put off by the fact that Virginia Woolf slated her brother-in-law's literary style; John Waller Hills' *A Summer on the Test* (1924) is a gem. Skues is a must; the most free-ranging and discursive of his titles is *Side-Lines, Side-Lights and Reflections* (1932). *Confessions of a*

Carp Fisher by Denys Watkins-Pitchford, author and illustrator, better known by his nom-de-plume 'BB', portrays the addiction to which the fanatic angler is prone with rare feeling. Henry Williamson's *Salar the Salmon* (1935) describes with intense feeling the life cycle of this great fish.

In order to understand what the fish itself is about, include Colonel E. W. Harding's *The Fly-Fisher and the Trout's Point of View* (1931) – then, and now, an underrated masterpiece on angling optics. For anyone with an interest in angling artists Walter Shaw Sparrow's *Angling in British Art* (1923) is essential. The best of entomological references is Martin Moseley's *Dry-Fly Fisherman's Entomology* (1921) though Alfred Ronalds' *Fly Fisher's Entomology* first published in 1836, should be alongside it. For gentle perception, unusual perhaps in a politician though not one who was to be such a fine Foreign Secretary, Sir Edward Grey's *Fly-fishing* (1899) demands inclusion. For the fine art of fly-dressing George Kelson's *The Salmon Fly* (1895) and for trout fly identification A. Courtney Williams' *Dictionary of Trout Flies* are essential. For the scholar's viewpoint on angling none seriously rival the second, revised edition of *Fishing from the Earliest Times* (1926) by William Radcliffe.

For one of the finest reads on salmon William Scrope's *Days and Nights of Salmon Fishing on the Tweed* (1843) is both poignant and pithy. Include W. C. Stewart's *The Practical Angler* (1857) for historical perspective; Andrew Lang's *Angling Sketches* (1891) for Scottish humour; J. W. Dunne's *Sunshine and the Dry Fly* (1924) for a brilliant mind applying itself to the age old angling problem of recreating translucency in the body of the natural fly; and any of Zane Grey's titles for the thrill of deep sea fishing. Halford must be included and of his seven titles, take the first, *Floating Flies and How to Dress Them* (1886). If you can find a copy and not lose an arm and a leg in the process take in T. C. Hofland's *The British Angler's Manual* (1839) for elegant charm.

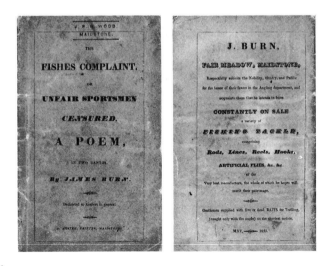

LEFT
A rare paperback published in 1843 and written by James Burn. It carries a most graceful-ly worded advertisement on its back cover.

RIGHT
Publisher's promotion piece issued by A. & C. Black Ltd.

FAR RIGHT
Classic front cover design, 1946.

Last but one *Three Men in a Boat* (1889) – not an angling book in the true sense but a tale to delight all who revel in the waterside and the foibles of mankind as they can apply to anglers and add too for pure excitement John Buchan's *John MacNab* (1925).

Finally old Izaak Walton and his companion Charles Cotton. Take any edition of their masterpiece and joy is yours for hours, for, as William Hazlitt has written 'Walton's *Compleat Angler* is so full of naivete, of unaffected sprightliness, of busy trifling, of dainty songs, of refreshing brooks, of shady arbours, of happy thoughts, and of the herb called Heart's Ease!'

LEFT
Bookplates are now widely collected, though plates with angling as their theme are particularly rare. This example shows the bookplate of the Fly-fishers' Club of London.

BELOW
Bookmark advertising Mellin's Cod Liver Oil Emulsion.

Angling in Art

Angling is relatively poorly represented in British sporting art. Hunting, coaching, horseracing and shooting all have richer and more varied art to satisfy the collector. It is however not difficult to see why this should be so. Fishing was not a sport much favoured by the upper class until the late 17th or early 18th century – and even then it was a solitary sport, not much given to dramatic action. Patrons therefore were not so plentiful as for other sports in which commissions were generally more numerous.

The result has been that fishing pictures, because of their scarcity, have commanded very high prices over the years. That is a trend which is likely to continue, with many of the finest examples of fishing pictures sadly locked away in the basements and storerooms of our national and regional museums.

Fortunately a wider representation of angling art is available through prints. At one time or another almost all the major sporting printmakers issued series of angling prints either individually, or in books. Many have survived to the present day recording the calm and tranquillity so often associated with angling as well as the thrill of the encounter with the fish once it has taken the lure.

Notably, a number of famous artists have themselves been anglers. The following for example, was written about the great J. M. W. Turner R.A. by Dr William Russell:

'The sole relaxation which this remarkable man permitted himself, besides certain potations – but it was not till late in life that he at times over-indulged – was fishing. He might be seen wending his way to the river side, dressed in the oddest fashion – a flabby hat, ill-fitting green Monmouth-street coat, nankeen trousers much too short, and highlow boots, with a dilapidated cotton umbrella, and a fishing-rod. From early morning till nightfall would he sit upon the river's bank, under pelting rain, patiently, shielded by his capacious umbrella, even though he did not obtain a single nibble. He was not, however, an unskilful angler, and was very proud of a good day's sport. He often fished in the Thames at Brentford.'

BELOW
Portrait of Ernest Briggs RI (1866-1913). From a water-colour by A. T. Nowell.

RIGHT
This charming study of a small boy was found in a junk shop in West London with a finger pushed through the centre of his face.

Three Men in a Boat

The illustration below appeared in *Dramatic and Sporting News* and depicts scenes from *Three Men in a Boat* by Jerome K. Jerome. Launched on its way to fame and posterity in 1889, the book records a holiday on the Thames, some angling feats and many happy idylls along the way. This, perhaps specially for the angler, says it all: 'Let your boat of life be light, packed with only what you need – a homely home and simple pleasures, one or two friends worth the name, someone to love and someone to love you, a cat, a dog, and a pipe or two, enough to eat and enough to wear, and a little more than enough to drink; for thirst is a dangerous thing.'

ANGLING ILLUSTRATION

Untold joy is expressed in angling illustration. Over the years the fishing book has provided more commissions for artists and illustrators to work on angling subjects than any other single source.

On this page are shown examples of wood engravings by Agnes Miller Parker reproduced from H. E. Bates' *Down the River*, 1937, a book of which the *Observer* wrote in its review of 3 October, in that year, 'An essential work of reference to every student of real England'.

ANGLING ILLUSTRATION

Born in August 1753 at Cherryburn House, near Eltringham in Northumberland, Thomas Bewick was the eldest of eight children. He showed artistic talent from an early age and was apprenticed at 14 to a Newcastle engraver, specialising in the production of billheads. Unwilling to execute occasional printers' requests for wood engravings, his master left the work to Bewick who showed a remarkable aptitude for it. He spent a brief and unhappy spell in London after completing his apprenticeship but soon returned to his native Northumberland, opening a shop in Newcastle with his brother, from which he worked for the next 50 years. He died, aged 75, on 8 November 1828. He is perhaps best known for his woodcuts of animals and of birds. But his charming angling scenes, some of which are illustrated on this page, show that Bewick, himself an angler, was familiar with all the many predicaments of the sport.

Negley Farson was one of the greatest newspaper reporters of his age. He worked as a foreign correspondent, fishing in many out-of-the-way places. His classic *Going Fishing* was illustrated by the Cheshire artist C. F. Tunnicliffe.

Fish (fly-replete, in depth of June,
Dawdling away their wat'ry noon)
Ponder deep wisdom, dark or clear,
Each secret fishy hope or fear.

BELOW
'It was always a battle if they made for the reeds.'

from 'Heaven' by
Rupert Brooke

ABOVE
'Light-backed trout with vivid red spots.'

ANGLING ILLUSTRATION

Angling Studies drawn and
etched by William Henry Pyne
(1769-1843), an uncommonly
fine draughtsman.

I Spy

Of some 2,350 caricatures published in the weekly magazine *Vanity Fair* between 1869 and 1914 only two portrayed anglers. The Rt Hon. Sydney Buxton was Post-Master General when the illustration (RIGHT) appeared in 1907. The other angling Spy caricature (BELOW) was of William Black and was published on 21 February 1891.

SNAP

Almost every angling diary contains snapshots. The pictures (BELOW and RIGHT) are taken from the diary of Leonard de Smidt whose early life was spent as a water engineer on the Nile engaged in the building of the first Aswaan dam – which gave him more opportunities to shoot than to fish. He retired in 1925 and from then onwards fished almost every day on the River Exe during the salmon and trout season, with occasional sorties to the River Otter. In the winter, during the Exe close season, he fished daily for pike in the Exeter Canal.

The legend on the back of the picture (BELOW LEFT) reads 'Tom's come Home after Katching these Big trout in a Little Brook that runs just from Shire Weir. It waid 3lbs and mashered 21 inches.'

BELOW
A 165lb Nile Perch caught at Aswaan in May 1924 annotated 'A Record Fish'.

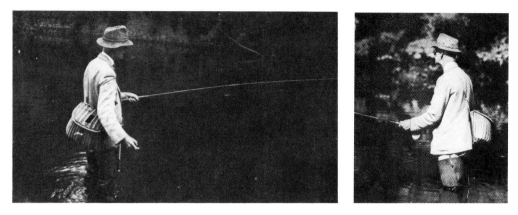

A noted Exe fisherman, Leonard de Smidt, below Tiverton Castle in 1943.

LEFT
This trout was caught by a Mr Warner on the Exe at Tiverton and was later sent to the Exeter Museum. It weighed 9lb 3oz.

LEFT
A well proportioned pike, photographed in its glass case by its captor.

GAMES ANGLERS PLAY

Perhaps the commonest game played by the budding young angler is 'Sardines'. That apart, 'The Happy Game of Flounders' figured prominently in children's toy cupboards from Victorian times onwards. There were many variants of this, though the basics were the same. A piece of cardboard which opened into a square, depicting on the outside different fish, cutouts of the fish themselves, all numbered, which were placed inside the box on the floor – and a series of rods with string fixed at the end, either with a hook on them to hook the fish's nose, or more usually with a magnet. The contestant was not allowed to look, turns were taken successively and the angler with highest score at the end was deemed the winner. Many manufacturers proudly advertised the game in their catalogues, doubtless to reassure ageing aunts, 'without water'.

Over the years Gamages' catalogues were filled with games for the off-duty angler to play. A clockwork Gold Fish, for the serious angler, might be considered a bit flippant, but what better for the bath than a clockwork swimming fish – or even grander, a diving fish? 'Dangle', the 'most realistic fishing game,' was one of many versions of the game of 'Flounders' to be advertised by Gamages between 1900 and 1940.

Clockwork Gold Fish.
No. 3261. 10½d. Post 2d.

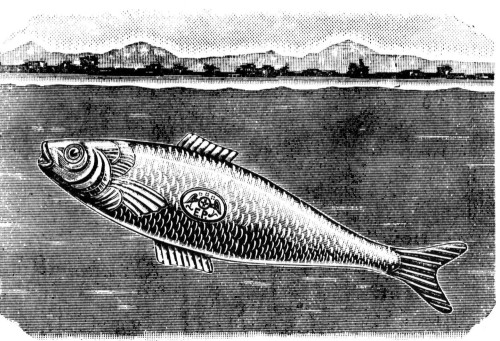

'Jumping Trout', a game of skill indeed. The anglers take turns, score 15 if they land a fish, five if they hook one and it comes off. The trout are hinged at the centre with a mousetrap-like device which literally flips the fish into the air when it is successfully hooked.

ANGLING IN PUNCH

Can the number of times angling crops up as a subject in *Punch* cartoons, be taken as a pointer to the popularity of the sport at any given moment?

In fact, on a count, angling scores rather less well than hunting and shooting in the 1880s and '90s and thereafter significantly less well than golf. Perhaps that tells more about the readers of *Punch* than about the popularity of angling as a participant sport.

In any event, *Punch* does provide a persistent record of the foibles of angling as seen by the general public over all these years.

GEORGE DU MAURIER (1831–1896).

ENCOURAGING PROSPECT!

Piscator Juvenis : " Any sport, sir ?"
Piscator Senex : " Oh, yes ; very good sport."
Piscator Juvenis : " Bream ?"
Piscator Senex : " No ! "
Piscator Juvenis : " Perch ?"
Piscator Senex : " No ! "
Piscator Juvenis : " What sport, then ?"
Piscator Senex : " Why, keeping clear of the weeds."

LEFT
'A Day with the Fly' from *Punch*, 27 August 1919.

ABOVE
Petulant Angler. 'If you want me to catch my fish, for goodness' sake stop flashing that sandwich.' 2 July 1919.

ON THE CARDS

Of the hundreds of series of cigarette cards issued very few were exclusively devoted to fish. The series most commonly found are those produced by John Player & Sons of Bristol entitled 'Fresh-Water Fishes' and 'Sea Fishes'. 'Fresh-Water Fishes' was issued as a set of 50 cards in November 1933. It was re-issued as a set of 25 cards in a slightly larger format in June 1935. 'Sea Fishes' was issued as a set of 50 in November 1935. Cards had lightly gummed backs for sticking into preprinted booklets. The notes accompanying the cards were supplied by R. L. Marston, editor of the *Fishing Gazette* and Sidney Spencer, a well-known sea trout angler and author.

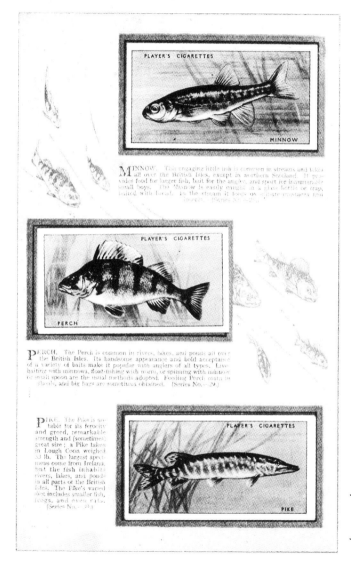

THE COMMON TROUT

ABOVE

Jumbo-sized cigarette cards were quite rare. This card is from a series of 25 issued by John Player & Sons in 1932 entitled 'Aquarium Studies'.

ON THE CARDS

Henry, 'enfant terrible', appeared in numerous guises on cards issued free with Kensitas cigarettes. Carl Anderson, his creator, was clearly no stranger to the torments and foibles of anglers. Five series of Henry cards were issued between July 1935 and March 1937.

The cigarette cards (RIGHT) are from the series 'Sea Fishes' by John Player & Sons Ltd. It proved one of their most popular series.

W. and F. Faulkner issued the cards illustrated (RIGHT) as a set of 25 entitled 'Angling' in January 1929. It was however earlier issued as a set by another cigarette manufacturer, Stephen Mitchell and Son of Glasgow in 1928. The set illustrates important fishing waters – game, coarse and sea venues being included.

Cards from an unusual series of 25, Rod and Gun, issued by William Ruddell of Dublin in 1924.

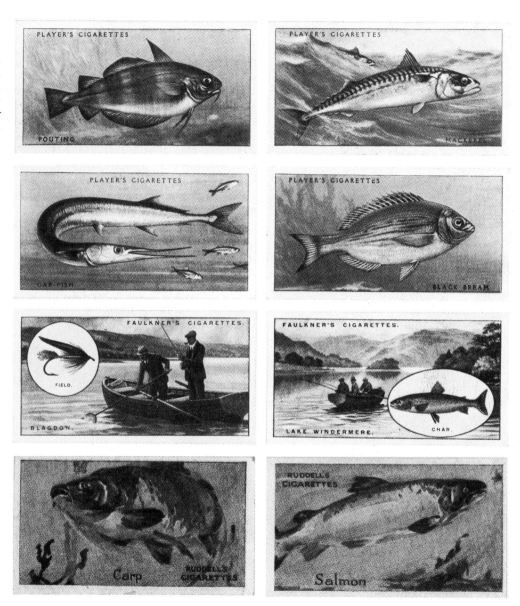

THE ANGLER'S MAIL

It has been estimated that between 1900 and 1914, no less than two million postcards, each bearing a ½p stamp, were passing through the post *each day*. With such a vast output, it is not surprising that a fair number of postcards should have had angling themes throughout this period. Indeed as recorded elsewhere in this book, every conceivable disaster or mishap which could befall the fisherman – as well as a good many triumphs too – were recorded in postcards over the years.

Almost as rewarding as the cards themselves are the messages on the back, especially if they record an equal disaster – or a triumph.

The reason why so many cards have survived is because recipients often stored them in ready-made postcard albums which were widely available from around 1900 onwards. The disadvantage however is that, as cards were invariably retained in a slot cut in the page by their corners, many cards were damaged in inserting or subsequently removing them.

An Absent-minded Beggar

A Valentine's postcard of 1912 captioned 'An Absent-minded Beggar'.

Stamps of the 1930s. Purists might perhaps not approve the Guianan Indians' angling technique.

ABOVE LEFT
'Now then John, move up'. A satirical card by Arthur Moreland, posted on 5 January 1904, and issued by C. W. Faulkner.

RIGHT
A remarkable likeness to Peter Sellers. Fish like these in silver foil, usually made of chocolate, were commonly given as gifts in France.

Terrors of the Pier!

LEFT

Misch & Co's 'On the Pier' series No 432.

BELOW

This card was published by Raphael Tuck in their Oilette series and is by the brilliant cartoonist Phil May. It is captioned: Clergyman . . . 'My boy, do you know that it's wicked to fish on the Sabbath?' Youngster . . . 'I isn't fishin' – I'm teachin' this 'ere wurm ter swim!'

Nos poissons de nos cœurs, sont les doux émissaires
Vous portant, en ce jour, nos vœux les plus sincères

CLERGYMAN : "My boy, do you know that it's wicked to fish on the Sabbath?"
YOUNGSTER : "I isn't fishin'—I'm teachin' this 'ere wurm ter swim !"

THE ANGLER'S MAIL

Raphael Tuck & Sons published this, one of the most elegant series of angling postcards. They were printed from paintings by the well-known angling artist A. Roland Knight and issued under the title 'British Fish' as 'Oilette' series No 3288. These four cards were captioned 'Trout – Hooked but not Landed'; 'Spinning for Pike – "Got him"'; 'Salmon – The First Leap'; 'Salmon – Landed'.

The 'Oilette' range of cards was first launched in 1903. They were well-designed, impeccably printed cards, each reproduced from an original painting – one incidentally which Tucks themselves had usually commissioned. Oilettes were normally sold in a pack of six, which came in an envelope embellished with such advertising slogans as 'Are Used by Royalty'. This indeed was no idle boast as Tucks held the Royal Warrant as suppliers of postcards to HM the King and Queen. The two other cards in this set showed a trout about to be drawn up in a landing net and somewhat incongruously a leaping black bass.

A BIT OF A SCRAP

Production of scraps – or 'printed embossed reliefs' as they were known to the trade, increased dramatically in the 1880s and 1890s. Standards of production rose too with the development of lithographic printing and steam driven embossing and stamping presses. Indeed to ensure the highest quality, up to 20 colours were used in printing some designs.

Scraps were sold in large sheets to be cut up and pasted individually into the collector's album. The practice however of breaking up sheets meant that it is now unusual ever to find complete 'sets' as originally issued. As the small ladders connecting scraps, which were cut away, bore the trademark and pattern number of the manufacturing company, identification of scraps too is difficult.

Angling appears seldom to have featured as a theme but does crop up occasionally in series covering other sports and trades.

One, two, three, four, five
Once I caught a fish alive
Six, seven, eight, nine, ten
Then I let him go again.
'Why did you let him go?'
'Because he bit my finger so'
'Which finger did he bite?'
'Why, this little finger on the
    right'.

BELOW
This scrap was the trade mark, copyrighted in 1884, of Scott's Emulsion of pure cod liver oil. Scott's Emulsion was advertised under the slogan 'Palatable as milk'. The codfish, which weighed 156lbs, was caught off the coast of Norway. The manufacturer claimed that this illustration was 'taken from life'.

A fine scrap published by D. S. Israel of Berlin who specialised in large tableaux format. It appears that copyright in scraps may not have been well protected as almost identical style and subject matter was used by M. Priester's Continental Printing Company of London and Berlin who had issued a series of 12 scraps entitled 'British Sports and Pastimes' between 1887 and 1889.

A Bit of a Scrap

This unusual series of scraps was devoted mostly to methods of commercial fishing and poaching. It nevertheless shows an angler precariously poised, with a fish coming up to be gaffed. Probably produced by Raphael Tuck & Sons whose output of scraps, as so much other printed material, was prodigious.

A fragment from a charming coloured group incongruously including both sea and fresh-water fish, as well as a sword-fish and a turtle. Entitled 'Fish and Crustacea', the centrepiece was a splendid lobster. The sheet, which measured 330mm × 245mm was originally published by Birn Brothers of London, who traded from 1882-1914, and was printed in Germany. It was sold as design No 844 without identifying any fish. The example above does designate fishes names and appears to be a later issue.

CHRISTMAS IS A-COMING

Angling, always in a very sentimental context, figures occasionally
in early Victorian Christmas cards.

STOP ME AND BUY SOME

Manufacturers' trade cards similarly used angling themes. RIGHT is a card distributed by J. & P. Coats, the cotton and thread manufacturer, to customers in 1880. The card carried a calendar for that year on the reverse and advertised 'Best Six Card Spool Cotton for Sale by all Dealers in Dry Goods and Notions'.

As it is, incongruously, the admiring lady seated beside the fisherman has a box of spools of thread by her feet, presumably to throw at the fish!

J. & P. COATS' THREAD IS STRONG !

Perhaps an even more appropriate caption for the card LEFT would have been the verse which follows by John Donne – about whom Isaak Walton wrote his first book:

'Come live with me and be my
           love,
And we will some new
         pleasures prove
Of golden sands, and crystal
         brooks,
With silken lines, and silver
         hooks.'

RIGHT
Alas! The child who sleeps unwisely but all too well. This card was issued by Frear's 'wide-awake house-keeping dep't' at Troy Bazaar. The reverse advertised 'Fans and Parasols'.

VISIT FREAR'S WIDE-AWAKE HOUSE-KEEPING DEP'T, AND SAVE MONEY ON ALL YOUR PURCHASES OF TABLE LINEN, TOWELS, NAPKINS, QUILTS, TABLE AND PIANO COVERS, &c. TROY BAZAAR.

THE ANGLER'S TROPHY

Popular belief would have it that there are three stages in an anglers' development. The first stage is when the objective is to catch the most fish, succeeded in turn by the second, which is when the overriding ambition becomes to catch the largest fish. Final maturity is reached, or so it is said, when this phase is overtaken by the intention only to catch the most difficult fish.

It should be recorded that it is given to a few anglers – a *very* few – to succeed in catching not only the most large fish but from the most difficult places as well. Surprisingly such anglers are not always the most welcome in the clubhouse or at the annual dinner. Such can be the jealousy, angler to angler, that the epithets can then suggest that it is the fisher, not the fish, who should head for the taxidermist!

LEFT
The Fishmonger, final recourse
for the failed angler, for over a
century.

From 'The Spodnoodle Papers' a series by
W. Heath Robinson, 1923.

THE ONE THAT GOT AWAY

He was an honest business man
For fifty weeks each year;
His word was good as any bond,
His judgment sound and clear;
He traded, bargained, bought and sold
With wisdom broad and deep –
And when he'd spent an honest day
Retir'd to honest sleep.

But once a year a madness comes
And seizes on this man
And shakes him up and inside out,
As only madness can.
And makes this good man's honest tongue
From Truth's dull pathway stray
To babble weird tales all about
The one that got away!

RIGHT
'Lost Him: By Jove, the Finest Fish I ever saw'. A Raphael Tuck postcard issued in their 'Connoisseur' series, No 2553. This card was chromotyped in Bavaria and posted in Rotherhithe at 10.15am on 22 September 1905.

TAILPIECE

The Cure.